LA PRIMERA

The Story of Wild Mustangs

IAN TYSON

Paintings by ADELINE HALVORSON

TUNDRA BOOKS

Published in Canada by Tundra Books,
75 Sherbourne Street, Toronto, Ontario M5A 2P9

Published in the United States by Tundra Books of Northern New York,
P.O. Box 1030, Plattsburgh, New York 12901

Library of Congress Control Number: 2008903006

Library and Archives Canada Cataloguing in Publication

Tyson, Ian, 1933-
    La primera : the story of wild mustangs / Ian Tyson ; Adeline Halvorson,
illustrator.

Based on lyrics of author's song with same title.
Accompanied by a CD
ISBN 978-0-88776-863-7

    1. Mustang–Juvenile poetry. 2. Children's poetry, Canadian (English).
3. Mustang–Juvenile literature. I. Halvorson, Adeline II. Title.

PS8639.Y86P75 2009   jC811'.6   C2008-902103-7

We acknowledge the financial support of the Government of Canada through the
Book Publishing Industry Development Program (BPIDP) and that of the
Government of Ontario through the Ontario Media Development Corporation's
Ontario Book Initiative. We further acknowledge the support of the Canada
Council for the Arts and the Ontario Arts Council for our publishing program.

ONTARIO ARTS COUNCIL
CONSEIL DES ARTS DE L'ONTARIO

The paintings for this book were rendered in acrylics on linen

Printed and bound in China

1 2 3 4 5 6   14 13 12 11 10 09

Dedicated to my mom, Peggy,
for instilling in me a love of horses,

and to my dad, Donald,
for creating a home where I could have a horse of my own.

– A.H.

La Primera

LA PRIMERA

It was a long hard voyage to the Americas in 1493
I was afraid that I would die of thirst
The little mare beside me died and was put into the sea
But I survived I swam to shore, I am La Primera

When Cortez sailed for Mexico from that island in the sun
There were sixteen of us sorrels, blacks, and bays
One of them my first born he was called the Coyote Dun
He survived, we conquered all of Mexico

Chorus:
I am a drinker of the wind I am the one who never tires
I love my freedom more than all these things
The Conquistador – Comanche and the Cowboy
I carried them to glory
I am La Primera – Spanish mustang hear my story

The Comanche were holy terrors when they climbed upon our backs
When the grass was green they would raid for a thousand miles
But the Texans had revolvers when they returned from the war
Buffalo had gone away the Comanche moon was waning

So it's come along boys and listen to my tale
We are following the longhorn cow going up Mister Goodnight's trail
You see those Cowboys were kind to us
We listen to their sad songs all the way to the far Saskatchewan

Chorus:
High in the Pryor Mountains
First light of dawn
Coyote Dun walks beneath the Morning Star
He became an outlaw . . . his blood was watered some
But the flame still burns into the new millennium

It was a long, hard voyage to the Americas in 1493.

I was afraid that I would die of thirst.

The little mare beside me died and was put into the sea.

But I survived. I swam to shore.

I am *La Primera.*

When Cortez sailed for Mexico
from that island in the sun,

there were sixteen of us –
sorrels, blacks, and bays.

One of them my firstborn;
he was called the Coyote Dun.

He survived, and we conquered all of Mexico.

I am a drinker of the wind. I am the one who never tires.
I love my freedom more than all these things: the conquistador,
Comanche, and the cowboy.

I carried them to glory.
I am La Primera – Spanish mustang – hear my story.

The Comanche were holy terrors
when they climbed upon our backs.

When the grass was green,
they would raid for a thousand miles.

But the Texans had revolvers
when they returned from the war.

The buffalo had gone away,
and the Comanche moon was waning.

So it's come along, boys, and listen to my tale.

We are following the longhorn cow,
going up Mister Goodnight's trail.

You see, those cowboys were kind to us.

We listened to their sad songs
all the way to far Saskatchewan.

High in the Pryor Mountains, at the first light of dawn,
Coyote Dun walks beneath the morning star.

He became an outlaw – his blood was watered some –
but the flame still burns into the new millennium.

WILD MUSTANGS

Ancestors of the modern horse were native to North America up until the end of the last Ice Age, about eight thousand years ago. Then, for reasons that are still unclear, they vanished from North America, while their relatives flourished in other parts of the world. The wild horses found in the western United States today have lived in North America for just five centuries. In the early 1500s, Spanish explorers arrived in search of wealth and power. They brought everything they needed to succeed in and conquer the New World, including their highly valued horses. A mixture of Andalusian, Arabian, and Barb, these animals had been bred for their beauty, strength, and speed. Those that survived the voyages and shipwrecks pulled supply carts, sped messengers to their destinations, helped ranchers tend their cattle, and carried conquering Spanish conquistadors into battle.

The Spanish horses flourished in their new home and grew more numerous. Every so often, a few escaped and ran free. Such renegades were called *mesteño* by the Spanish, meaning "stray animal." Over time, the Spanish word evolved into the English word *mustang*. Wild herds formed and were

joined by other breeds introduced by European settlers, who had also come to make their fortunes.

For three hundred years or so, the Spanish and European horses interbred and adapted to the western grasslands from Mexico to Canada. By the mid 1800s, there were between two and four million wild mustangs, bearing little resemblance to the beautiful Spanish horses from which they had descended. They had become hardier, smaller, more compact, keenly intelligent, and sure-footed. These were the qualities needed to survive the harsh environment and avoid areas inhabited by humans.

Mustangs had a profound effect on Native American culture. When the Spanish first arrived with their horses, the Indians had never seen such powerful, swift, and terrifying beasts. But as time passed, they grew to understand the great value of horses and learned to capture and subdue wild mustangs of the western plains. Horses quickly became prized possessions and valuable items of trade. Indians proved themselves to be excellent riders and, with the help of their horses, were able to expand their territories and hunt with greater ease. Horses that were traded from tribe to tribe eventually contributed to the further spread of wild mustangs.

By the 1900s, mustang herds began to shrink as ranchers and settlers moved west, bought land, and put up fences. Grazing lands were now reserved for growing numbers of cattle, while mustangs were forced into less desirable, more remote areas. Ranchers who viewed feral horses as a major problem, shot as many as possible and, in some states, even offered rewards for each mustang killed.

Mustangs were not considered a nuisance by everyone, however. To some, mustangs were seen as a resource. They were captured and sold overseas to satisfy the wartime demand for horses, particularly for use in the Boer War and World War I. Whether through culling or capture, the number of feral horses dwindled. By the 1920s, their population was estimated to be only one million.

The plight of the dwindling herds angered many people, but in particular a woman named Velma Johnston who lived near Reno, Nevada. She campaigned to alert the public about the atrocities suffered by the horses and persuaded the government to pass a law making it illegal to use airplanes or vehicles to round up and capture mustangs on public lands. But Velma's victory was not enough. The numbers of wild horses continued to shrink, and by 1967, it was estimated that only thirty-five thousand of these magnificent animals remained. Velma Johnston continued her fight and, with the help of humane societies and horse protection organizations across the country, continued to press the government for full protection of the horses. She even organized a letter-writing campaign for school children throughout the nation and, with their help, convinced the government to pass the Wild Free-Roaming Horse and Burro Act in 1971. This law prohibited the capture for slaughter of wild horses and burros. The law also charged the Bureau of Land Management (BLM) in the Department of Interior with managing, controlling, and protecting mustang herds. In just one decade, their numbers increased by twenty thousand.

Today, with the government helping to protect wild horses, the growing herds have once again become a problem. There is not enough grazing land and water to support the mustangs and the ranchers' livestock. In an effort to keep the mustang population at an acceptable size, the Bureau of Land

Management has instituted the "Adopt-a-Horse" program, in which mustangs are captured and sold to qualified people who can provide proper care and homes for them.

The government's efforts to control the mustang population are marked by controversy. Cattle ranchers and others associated with the cattle industry continue to argue that the horses are a foreign species in the environment and that they compete with cattle for pasture land. Supporters of the mustangs argue that they pre-date modern ranching practices and have as much a right to be on public lands as cattle, which also happen to be a species foreign to North America.

The Bureau of Land Management estimates there are now fewer than thirty-seven thousand remaining wild horses. The majority can be found in Nevada and Wyoming. Smaller populations can be found in Idaho, Colorado, Arizona, and New Mexico. One select group of about one hundred twenty horses lives in the rugged Pryor Mountains of Montana, where they are carefully protected. Blood samples from these animals trace their origins all the way back to the original Spanish mustangs honored in Ian Tyson's song "La Primera." They are symbols of freedom and the pioneer spirit of the West, admired for their beauty, and, at long last, valued for their remarkable history.